GREAT SOCCER: Team Defense

Suzanne Cope

HIGH
interest
books

Children's Press
A Division of Scholastic Inc.
New York / Toronto / London / Auckland / Sydney
Mexico City / New Delhi / Hong Kong
Danbury, Connecticut

Thanks to Carlos Giron and the girls soccer team of St. Thomas Aquinas High School, Ft. Lauderdale, FL and Steve Lorenc and the boys soccer team of Piper High School, Sunrise, FL.

Book Design: Christopher Logan
Contributing Editor: Matthew Pitt
Photo Credits: Cover and all other photos by Maura Boruchow and Cindy Reiman; pp. 4, 6 © Temp Sport/Corbis

Visit Children's Press on the Internet at:
http://publishing.grolier.com

Library of Congress Cataloging-in-Publication Data

Cope, Suzanne.
    Great soccer : team defense / Suzanne Cope.
       p. cm. — (Sports clinic)
    Includes bibliographical references and index.
    ISBN 0-516-23166-9 (lib. bdg.) — ISBN 0-516-29562-4 (pbk.)
    1. Soccer—Defense—Juvenile literature. [1. Soccer.] I. Title. II. Series.

GV943.9D43 C66 2001
796.334'2—dc21

00-066049

CONTENTS

INTRODUCTION

Millions of women and men in Europe and South America consider it their favorite game. Here in the United States, we're finally learning how much fun the game is. What game? Soccer! Soccer is one of the few team sports played all around the world. Lately, Americans have joined in on the fun. These days, you probably could find a group of teams in your hometown.

Each soccer team has eleven players on each side. The object of the game is to score goals on the other team while keeping them from scoring goals on you. It can be a great thrill to stop the opposing team from scoring on your net. Good team defense can make the difference between victory and loss.

This book introduces the roles of different players on a team. You'll learn strategies, or plans, that will help you become a better defensive player. You'll also learn defensive drills you can practice with a friend, a group of friends, or on your own. The more you practice, the sooner these drills will become skills. Once you learn the skills, you'll have a leg up on the other players!

By blocking the shot, this goaltender helps lead his team to victory.

MEET YOUR TEAM

Soccer teams have four different positions: forwards, midfielders, defenders, and goalkeepers. This chapter examines the roles each position plays in a soccer game.

Forward

The main duty of a forward is to move the ball up the field and shoot at the other team's goal. Great forwards must have excellent dribbling and shooting skills.

Midfielder

A midfielder's job is to help the forwards score goals by passing and dribbling. Midfielders help the defense stop the other team from scoring, too. Midfielders usually are excellent runners and can pass the ball well.

Professional soccer players are great athletes. They must keep their bodies in top shape.

Defender

The duty of a defender is to keep the other team from scoring goals. Defenders must be aggressive. They must be able to think and move very quickly. They also must be able to take the ball away from the other team's talented forwards. The drills in Chapters 2 and 3 will help you along.

The best defenders shadow ev move their opponents make

FUN FACT:

People in countries such as Mexico, France, and Ireland call soccer by another name: football. Of course, it's very different from our version of football. They call the game football because players mainly move the ball around the field with their feet.

A team's goalkeeper is the last line of defense.

Goalkeeper

If a ball gets past the defense, it's up to the goal-keeper to stop it. Goalkeepers usually are called by their shortened name, goalies. Goalies are the only players who can touch the ball with their hands. They can use their hands only in the large goal box in front of the goal. The goal box area is marked with white, painted lines. Goalies must have strong leaping abilities. They also need good reflexes to stop the ball from getting past their fast hands.

Formation

Depending on your opponent's strength, your coach may use different mixes of players, or formations. Against a team with a strong offense, a coach may use a four-player defensive formation. This defense includes two defenders—one on each side, or wing, of the field. The formation also includes a stopper and a sweeper. A stopper "attacks" players trying to cross into his or her half of the field. Attack in this context means challenging the player with the ball by using just the feet. The stopper usually plays around the center of the field.

If the ball gets past the stopper, the two wing defenders will try to regain it. The wings attack any player who gets past the stopper on their side

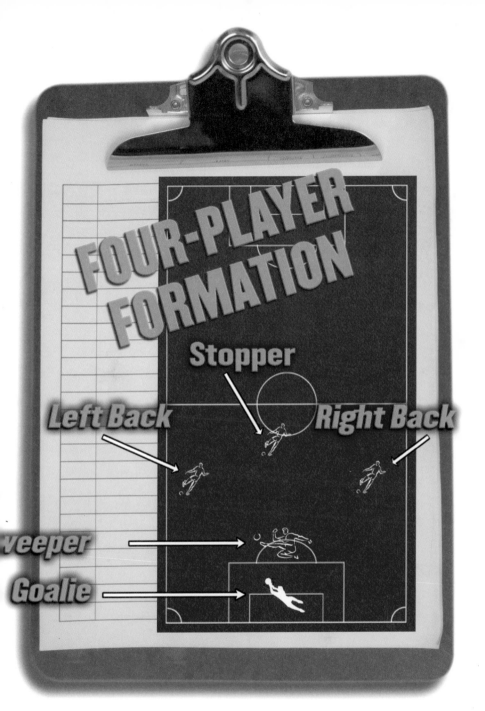

FOUR-PLAYER FORMATION

Stopper

Left Back

Right Back

Sweeper

Goalie

FUN FACT:

What's in a name? Each soccer position has a nickname. Another name for a forward is a striker. Midfielders are known as halfbacks, and defenders sometimes are called fullbacks.

of the field. If the wings are beaten as well, the sweeper cleans up behind them. Defense strategy can get very complicated! However, by communicating with your teammates and learning the drills, you'll catch on fast.

Pick Your Position

All the position players work together to try to win the game. Which position do you think would be right for you? If you feel you'd make a strong goalie or defender, read on!

DEFENSIVE SKILLS

Tackling

When you attack a forward or midfielder with the ball, you must tackle him or her to get the ball away. Tackling in soccer is not like tackling in American football. There are two types of tackling. When you attack, your opponent may try to pass the ball or move around you. If he or she makes a mistake, you can take advantage of it and take the ball away. That's one form of tackling. Other times, the offensive player will hold the ball still. He or she may be preparing to shoot or pass. When this happens, you must make a move and challenge your opponent for the ball. A lot of tackling success depends on how you position your body. You should use good form, or technique. Stay light on your feet. When you face your opponent, don't get caught flat-footed! Always be ready to spring into action. Stay in front of the

This defender is in a good position to tackle.

player with the ball. When you see an opportunity, stick your foot in and make the steal. Be ready for the opposing forward or midfielder to kick the ball too far when dribbling. Then it's your job to sprint to the ball and get there first.

Be careful not to get tricked into going the wrong way. Good forwards will try to use change-of-direction moves. This means that they pretend to go in one direction and then move the ball in another direction. Learn to read the forwards when they dribble. A great defender won't fall for many fakes. Yet no matter how much you practice, it's impossible to guess a forward's moves all the time.

The best fullbacks won't get fooled by fakes.

Sometimes defenders must tackle the ball from the side.

When both you and the opposing player are running down the field, you must tackle the ball from the side. It is only legal to tackle from the side when you have shoulder-to-shoulder contact with your opponent. As a defender, you're not allowed to take the ball from behind or use your hands. If you do, you'll get called for a foul. Keep in pace with your opponent. If he or she is dribbling down the sideline, try to kick the ball to the right or left. It's considered a good move to kick the ball out of bounds to stop the play.

Drills for Your Skills
By Yourself

While you can't practice tackling an offensive player by yourself, you can practice being in the correct position. Try small kicks to your right and left, keeping the ball near your feet. Stay on your toes, moving quickly from side to side. Keep your center of gravity—most of your body weight—low by bending slightly at the waist and knees.

These defenders practice correct tackling form.

With a Friend

Practice playing one-on-one with a friend. Have him or her dribble around you while you try to take the ball away. When you win the ball, switch roles. Let your friend practice defense. This will help improve both your tackling and dribbling skills.

To practice tackling from the side, give your friend a head start with the ball. Have your friend dribble toward the goal. Catch up with him or her. Try to take the ball away before he or she has a chance to shoot on goal. As you get better at this

In this drill the defender gives his friend a head start with the ball. He then sprints to catch up and get the ball back.

This defender is ready to make a great steal.

drill, challenge yourself. Give your friend a longer head start, or have him or her run closer to the goal. That way you have less time to catch your friend before he or she can get a clear shot.

Clearing

Often, a defender must get rid of the ball quickly. Perhaps players from the other team are closing in. Maybe no other defenders are in the area to protect the goal. When these situations occur, a defender has to clear the ball. This means kicking it away from his or her end of the field up to the midfielders or the forwards.

If the ball's rolling toward you, you should use the one-touch technique. To accomplish this, plant your non-kicking foot to the side of the ball. Face the direction you want the ball to travel in. Then, make solid contact with the center of the ball, kicking with the inside of your foot.

Sometimes clearing the ball involves more skills. If the ball is flying through the air, you must first "trap" it before you can pass. Trapping is when you stop the path of the ball. Once the ball is under control, it's easier to kick. You can trap the ball with your head, chest, legs, or feet. When you trap, move your entire body in front of the ball. After you make contact, let your body give, or

One of the keys to a good clearing kick is making solid contact with the soccer ball.

relax, a little. This way the ball will stop instead of bouncing away. Think of a ball kicked against a wall. It bounces right off because the wall is rigid. However, if that same ball is kicked at the goal's net, it comes to a stop. That's because the net is much less rigid. So by making your body less rigid, you'll find the ball easier to play. Once you've trapped the ball, you then can clear it.

When clearing the ball, try aiming for a team-mate on the other side of the field. If you don't have time to aim, kick toward the sidelines instead of the center of the field.

Drills for Your Skills
By Yourself
Throw the ball into the air and practice trapping it with different parts of your body. Try to get the ball near your feet and ready to kick up the field quickly.

When you're trapping the ball, allow your body to give a little.

With a Friend

Have your friend stand about 10 yards away from you. Practice long, accurate kicks to him or her. Practice trapping the ball as well as using the one-touch technique.

Have a friend throw the ball in the air toward you and practice trapping the ball and kicking it back. Have another friend or a coach time how long it takes you to trap and kick.

Soccer players should learn to trap with several parts of their bodies.

THREE

GUARDING
THE GOAL

Goalkeeping

The goalie is the last line of defense on a soccer team. A goalie must have special skills, different from those of other teammates. For example, having quick hands is very important. A goalie must be ready to dive on a ball the instant it's kicked toward the net. He or she must be able to jump high to block shots headed for the upper part of the goal. Finally, goalies need to have lightning-quick reflexes.

Once the goalie controls the ball, he or she can throw it to a teammate or drop-kick it up the field. A drop-kick occurs when the goalie drops the ball from his or her hands on to an extended foot, kicking it far up the field. When you perform a drop-

This goalie's quick hands help him make the save.

kick, keep your center of gravity low and your eye on the ball until it makes contact with your foot. Don't throw the ball into the air. Instead, simply let it drop from your hands. The ball should make contact with your foot before touching the ground.

Penalty Kicks

If a defender makes a foul in his or her own goal box area, a penalty kick is called. Fouls that lead to penalty kicks include tripping or pushing an opponent. If the referee calls a penalty kick, it's up to the goalie to stop the shot. He or she gets no help from the other defenders.

During a penalty kick, the referee marks a spot 10 yards from the goal line. A forward on the opposing team then gets a free shot on goal. Goalies must react as soon as the ball is kicked and dive in the direction of the ball. It's hard to stop a penalty shot, but a practiced goalie can do it!

Goalies must react instantly to a penalty kick.

Drills for Your Skills
By Yourself

Practice your agility by moving quickly from one side of the goal to the other. Get comfortable moving laterally, or side to side. Throw the ball into the air and practice catching it. Practice your throwing and drop-kicking motions.

With a Friend

While you're seated on the ground, have a friend throw the ball to you. Have him or her also throw to your right and left. Try to stop the ball from getting past you. This helps improve your reflexes as well as your catching skills.

Practice your leaping ability. Have a friend throw the soccer ball toward the highest points of the goal. Even if you can't leap high enough to catch the ball, try to tip, or deflect, it.

Stand in position in the goal and have your teammates practice shooting the ball from different areas in front of the goal. Then, have your teammates practice penalty shots from the designated spot 10 yards from the goal line.

Great goalies are always aiming to improve their reflexes.

FOUR

GAME PLAN

Playing the Game

Now that we've covered tackling, trapping, and clearing, let's discuss how to put them to use in a game situation.

When an opponent takes the ball into your half of the field, a defender must attack that player while the remaining defenders provide backup. If several players from the other team are running toward your half of the field, midfielders must come back and help "mark-up." This means that each midfielder and defender on your side covers one opposing player on offense.

This strategy works especially well when your opponent has a "throw-in" from the sidelines. Throw-ins occur when a team kicks the ball out of bounds along the sideline. When this happens, the opposing team is allowed to throw the ball from the sideline. Throwers must keep both feet

Once a defender learns new skills, he or she can put them to use in a game.

on the ground, hurling the ball from behind the head with both hands. To keep an opponent from getting the ball, a defender must stay close to the person he or she is marking. If the opponent does get the ball, it's the defender's job to tack-le that player and get the ball back for the team.

Offside

A rule that helps defenders is the offside rule. It states that an offensive player can't receive the ball when there aren't at least two defenders (including the goalie) between the offensive player and the net. If an opponent does get the ball in this situation, he or she is offside. If an offensive player is caught offside, the defense gets a free

One of a defender's main duties is to get the ball back for the team.

kick—the opportunity to kick the ball up the field toward the other goal. This is a tricky rule—have a coach explain it again if you have any questions.

A good defense will try to draw, or catch, the other team offside. This is done by "pushing up" the defense when an opponent lags behind. Pushing up means moving the entire defense toward the other end of the field. The sweeper usually decides whether to push up or not. If the strategy is successful, the offensive player will get called for the penalty and the defense will get the ball back.

Minding the Net

A goalie's strategy is to try to cut down the angle from where he or she thinks the ball will be shot. A good goalie does this by turning to face the kicker when the kicker is to the right or left of the goal. The goalie then will move forward a few feet toward that side of the goal. This strategy makes

This goalie is prepared for the kicker's shot.

the kicker's target much smaller. However, a goalie must learn not to come too far outside the goal area. If that happens, the forward simply may dribble around the goalie and score into the empty net. Practicing will help you learn a good balance.

When the ball goes past the goal line (the boundary line on either end of the field), either a goal kick or a corner kick is called. When the offense kicks it out, the defense will have a goal kick. If you're selected to kick the goal kick, you may place the ball anywhere on the goal box line. Use a long, clearing kick. Try to pass to a team-mate. If you're not the kicker, move around to get open. If you're unguarded, the kicker will aim his or her pass to you.

If your team kicks the ball out of bounds along the goal line, your opponent will take a corner kick. This is a free kick placed at the corner of the field. When that happens, defenders must mark up every opponent in the area. Also, the wing defender should stand next to the goal post near-est the corner kick.

Final Words

Now you've learned the basics of soccer—so get out there and play! If you'd like to join a team, try contacting your school or local recreation center. Usually they have organized teams or leagues. Many cities also have professional or college soccer teams. Get tickets to a game—they're fun to watch! Then you can try to recognize all the moves and skills that you've learned.

Practice is an important part of soccer, and no one gets better without it. Always practice your skills correctly so that they'll be second nature when it's game time. Put every ounce of your effort into the game. When you and an opposing player both race for the ball, don't give up! Also, try to visualize what the opposing team will do next. Does that player with the ball like to pass or shoot? Is everyone on your side marking the right player? You're a better defender when you can guess the opponent's next move.

Lastly—and most importantly—play by the rules. No goal is worth hurting the other team or cheating. Respect the other team. If it's better than yours, don't lose your temper. Instead, use that energy to work and practice even harder. The great thing about soccer is that anyone can learn to play and everyone can improve. Respecting yourself, your teammates, and the other team is the first step in becoming a great defender and player.

After a game, always remember to congratulate your opponent.

change-of-direction when a player pretends
to go one way and then kicks the ball in
another direction

defenders players who try to stop the other
team from scoring

dominant stronger

dribbling kicking the ball just ahead of your feet

formation the combination of different positions
on the field

forwards players whose main job is to shoot and
score at the opposing team's goal

goalkeepers players responsible for guarding the
net from the opposing team's shots

leading passing or throwing the soccer ball
ahead of a teammate

mark-up when each defender covers one opponent on the other team

midfielders players who set up goals by passing the ball to the forwards

offside a rule that an offensive player may only play the ball when there are at least two defenders between him or her and the goal

opponents players on another team

shooting kicking the ball toward the goal in an attempt to score

strategies plans

tackling taking the ball away from an offending player

trapping stopping the ball with your body

FOR FURTHER READING

Anderson, Dave. *The Story of the Olympics.* New York: HarperCollins Publishers, 2000.

Christopher, Matt. *On the Field With Mia Hamm.* Boston: Little, Brown, and Company, 1998.

Weber, Chloe. *Mia Hamm Rocks!* New York: Welcome Rain Publishing, 1999.

Woods, Paula. *Improve Your Soccer Skills.* London: Usborne House, 1993.

Woog, Dan. *20 Steps to Better Soccer.* Chicago: Lowell House, 2000.

Organizations

Alliance of Youth Sports Organizations
P.O. Box 351
South Plainfield, NJ 07080

American Youth Soccer Organization (AYSO)
12501 South Isis Avenue
Hawthorne, CA 90250

RESOURCES

Web Sites

Soccer America

http://www.socceramerica.com/

The home page of *Soccer America* magazine, this Web site features a youth link along with information about soccer camps and the U.S. National team.

Internet Soccer

http://internetsoccer.com/

This Web site gives you links to soccer news from around the world. There's also a link that shows you what other youth soccer teams are doing.

INDEX

About the Author

Suzanne Cope is a freelance writer and avid soccer player who lives in Boston, Massachusetts. She has been playing soccer since she was 12 years old. Suzanne also coaches youth soccer and referees in her spare time. Her favorite position is fullback.